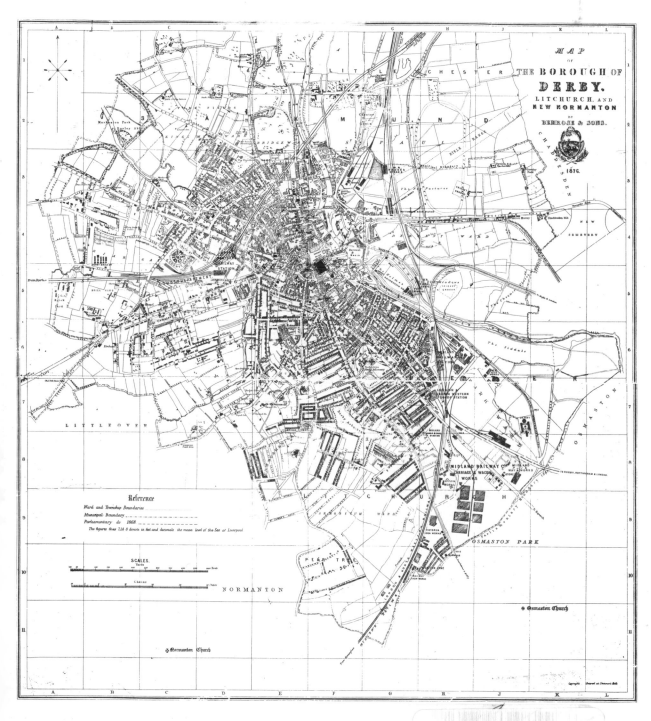

MAP
OF
THE BOROUGH OF
DERBY,
LITCHURCH, AND
NEW NORMANTON
BY
BEMROSE & SONS.
1876.

Reference
Ward and Township Boundaries
Municipal Boundary
Parliamentary do 1868
The figures thus 214·8 denote in feet and decimals the mean level of the Sea at Liverpool

SCALES.
Yards
Chains

Bygone
DERBY

Derby Guildhall, designed by Henry Duesbury, photographed *c*.1890.

Bygone
DERBY

Maxwell Craven

Phillimore

1989

Published by
PHILLIMORE & CO. LTD.
Shopwyke Hall, Chichester, Sussex

ISBN 0 85033 705 4

Printed and bound in Great Britain by
BIDDLES LTD.
Guildford, Surrey

List of Illustrations

Frontispiece: Derby Guildhall, *c*.1890

Illustration Acknowledgements

The author is grateful to the following for permission to reproduce illustrations: Anonymous, private collection, 38, 110, 129, 131, 146, 158, 168, 181b, 186; Author's collection, 5, 7, 14, 36, 55, 59, 125, 138, 173, 188b; C. H. Burton, 84; J. Darwin, 43; Derby City Council, 6, 20, 27, 46, 54, 87, 99, 100, 114, 117, 137, 143, 152, 178; Derby Museum, Map, 2-4, 8-12, 15-19, 21-23, 28-35, 37, 42, 44, 45, 47-51, 53, 56-64, 66-70, 72, 73, 75, 77, 78, 80, 85, 86, 88-93, 95-98, 101-109, 112, 113, 115, 118-120, 121-124, 126-128, 130, 132, 133a, 133b, 134-136, 139-142, 144, 145, 148-150, 153-157, 159, 160, 162-167, 170-172, 174, 175, 177, 179, 181a, 183-5, 187-191; Derby School, 82, 83, 169; *Derbyshire Life and Countryside*, 52; Derbyshire Museum Service, 65; the late Richard Foreman, 79, 116; Mrs. Anne Haslam, 26; R. G. Hughes, 151; National Monument Record, 81; Natwest Bank PLC, 71; D. Plowman, 176; E. J. Saunders, R.I.B.A., 182; Messrs. Taylor, Simpson & Mosley, 192.

Introduction

Until the middle of the 20th century, Derby was a market and county town around which grew up, from the 18th century, the girdle of industry for which it has become well-known. Derby is known by most people in this country as a railway town, for its Rolls-Royce production, and as the centre for the manufacture of fine china. Yet through all this industrial achievement, recently embellished by the coming of Toyota to the site of the former municipal airport at Burnaston, Derby has never lost its comfortable small-town atmosphere or its role as a market centre. Derby ceased to be a county town over 25 years ago and in 1974 lost its status as a county borough (granted in 1888); these losses, however, have to some extent been compensated for by its elevation to a City by Royal Letters Patent in 1977. Its dual role as county capital and market town allowed Derby to develop from the Restoration as a centre for the fashionable of the shire, and bestowed

1. The Markeaton Brook, bordered by St John's Terrace, in the West End. This view was taken looking north-west and St John's church would be just to the left, off the picture. The large house in the middle distance was built in the 1870s as the vicarage. The Regency cottages bordering the street were built by Thomas and Joseph Cooper to house the employees of an adjacent mill. The scene is little changed today, over fifty years later.

upon it an elegant classical architectural heritage much of which has survived, despite the baleful influence of destructive post-war planning policies.

Before the coming of the Romans to Britain in A.D. 43, the site was, as far as we can tell, but sparsely inhabited. The borough later grew up on a low acclivity of land west of the Derwent, and was bounded on the south and west by a secondary stream, the Markeaton Brook, in ancient times a marshy area. From south to north ran an ancient trackway, following the course of the river, crossing the Markeaton Brook and ascending over the rising ground immediately to its north. About a mile north of the Brook crossing, the high ground fell away to the Derwent as a bluff, and it was here that the first units of the Roman army to reach the area – at the time a borderland between the territory of two British tribes, the *Coritani* to the south and the *Brigantes* to the north – built a fort which even today has been little studied. Its true extent and longevity are something of a mystery. About forty years later, however, a civil settlement had begun to grow up on the low-lying ground on the east bank of the Derwent, called by the Romans *Derventio*. This settlement was served by the lowest crossing-point over the Derwent, and pottery making and metal working sustained life there to a remarkably high standard. Excavations carried out over the last two decades have revealed evidence of sophisticated buildings, grand tombs – some of the plinth type, larger versions of which graced the Appian Way out of Rome – and extensive suburban development. In the later third century, the settlement's walls were rebuilt stoutly in stone to a height of at least twenty feet.

The most important of the network of roads which intersected at *Derventio* was that later known as Ryknield Street, running in general terms from south-west to north-east. Its course is reasonably clear through the north-western parts of the present city, and originally it must have reached the first-century fort via the old north-south spinal trackway. Later it was diverted across the Derwent, presumably by bridge, to the east of *Derventio*, at which point it turned north. Another road ran from Willoughby-on-the-Wolds via a ferry across the Trent at Sawley to *Derventio*, where it swung west, crossed the river on a reasonably well attested bridge en route for Chesterton via Rocester (Staffs.). The north-south trackway itself was adapted and improved, crossing the Trent towards Leicester *(Ratae Coritanorum)* on a spectacular causeway at Swarkestone six miles south of Derby. This causeway may indeed owe its origins to pre-Roman engineering.

Derventio may have controlled a considerable subdivision of Coritanian territory, which could be the key to what happened after the collapse of Roman administration in Britain. There is little archaeological evidence for the survival of *Derventio* as a settlement. Circumstantial evidence may suggest a contrary story, not confirmable by excavation due to damage by subsequent agriculture and building. Nothing is known of events during the century and a half before the advent of the Mercian Saxons along the river valleys from the east in around A.D. 550. Yet a group of adults of both sexes was found buried, some with wounds, under the floor of a late-Roman building just outside the east gate of the settlement. By the early part of the century following, the embryonic Kingdom of Mercia had been established with its early capital at Repton, eight miles to the south-west on the south bank of the Trent, just off Ryknield Street. During the following century and a half the area around *Derventio*, extending some way west of the Derwent and south to the Trent, became a large unitary Mercian Royal or noble estate, named Northworthy. This was scattered with small settlements from which ultimately grew villages, named in the Domesday record of 1086, many of which today have been absorbed by Derby as suburbs.

By about A.D. 800, a minster church had been established on a high point on the isthmus of land between the Markeaton Brook and the Derwent, a little way to the south of

2. Queen Street, looking north to St Alkmund's, the successor of the middle Saxon minster church. The alignment of the street, part of the pre-historic trackway which long preceded the settlement of Derby, veered round the church, to the left in this view. The stylish mid-Georgian house half way along on the left is that built for John Whitehurst by Joseph Pickford in 1764. The photograph was taken by Richard Keene, *c.*1870.

the original Roman fort. Its purpose was to house six canons whose role was to re-evangelise the local population, and it was dedicated to St Alkmund, a Northumbrian martyr-prince whose remains were re-interred here due to the invasion of Northumbria by the Vikings. Around this church grew up a very small community which served it, and the original spinal route curved around it to the west. Nearby, on the Markeaton Brook, another early church dedicated to St Werburgh, a Mercian princess, was without doubt the focus of one of the small setlements which constituted the Northworthy estate. This settlement, from later evidence, appears to have been called Wardwick, a name which survives as a street in modern Derby.

In 873-4, Mercia was overrun by the Danish Great Army, and the Danes controlled the Northworthy estate until 917 when Aethelflaeda of Mercia turned them out by force. From the account of this we learn that the Danes' headquarters in Northworthy was almost certainly the refurbished Roman defences of *Derventio*, renamed Little Chester by the Saxons, and the area immediately surrounding it, including St Alkmund's, had been renamed Derby, the first syllable probably being a contraction from the Roman name, itself based on the Celtic name of the river Derwent.

Yet it was not until 941 that the area was finally brought back under Saxon hegemony, and by this time a Saxon *burh* or small fortified town had been established just south of St Alkmund's, with a second minster church, dedicated to All Saints, and a mint. This, the new Derby, marks the beginning of the City as we know it, established its topography, and set the pattern for its future development.

By the time of the Domesday survey, it had shrunk somewhat from the position in 1066, when there had been over two hundred burgesses. However, there were at least eight parish churches by then, grouped along the spinal trackway. Most were undoubtedly founded by munificent townsfolk and pious landowners whose estates included portions of the town. Some of these landowners, indeed, were lords of estates created from the break-up of greater Northworthy by the Saxon kings after the defeat of the Danes. In later times, these same estates acted as a straitjacket which for a time restricted the potential expansion of the town in the earlier 19th century.

During the Middle Ages, Derby's prosperity, once it had managed to shake off a series of pre-Conquest ties with Nottingham, increased steadily, based on the processing of lead and wool, glovemaking and malting. Local government, established by a series of Royal Charters from *c.*1155, was early on linked to the wealth and power of some six monastic institutions within the town, the influence of which was a long time waning. Nevertheless, the Dissolution released much land into private hands, particularly those of the burgesses. Their influence was, however, swiftly replaced by that of the county magnates who built town houses and busied themselves in the affairs of the Borough.

In 1637 King Charles I granted a new Charter which established an annually-elected mayor in place of the two bailiffs who had held office hitherto. Five years later, the burgesses threw in their lot with Parliament and the town was occupied by Sir John Gell, Bt., of Hopton. Trade received a severe setback, as the town was for some time an island in a Royalist sea. Oddly, the citizens of Derby welcomed the Restoration with as much enthusiasm as they had embraced Parliament 18 years before, and this event marked the start of a great rebuilding of the town which continued for a generation and was financed by the county gentry to whose every requirement the tradesmen strove to cater. In its train this brought a dramatic rise in the standard of craftsmanship and innovation. George Sorocold in 1692 devised the first of many schemes which he subsequently undertook for several other English towns to provide water to all parts of the town to replace the five or so

3. A fragment of Derby's monastic legacy: this 16th-century brick building with earlier fabric is all that remains of the convent of St Mary de Pratis. Standing, appropriately, on Nuns Street in the West End, it is today in very poor condition, with its windows bricked in, being used as an industrial store.

medieval wells. The water was raised from the Derwent near St Michael's church and piped out from there. His system, and its elm pipes, remained operational until 1849. Robert Bakewell (1682-1754) was pre-eminent amongst local craftsmen for the quality of his wrought ironwork, and a host of others stand out as of exceptional local if not national merit.

In the 18th century Derby began to run in the van of the industrial revolution, but not before the tumultuous political events of the 1730s. These culminated in the traumatic days of 4-6 December 1745 when Prince Charles Edward Stuart, at the head of some eight thousand men, stayed in the town, taking in his quarters, the long-demolished Exeter House, the fateful decision to halt the Jacobite advance towards London and return to Scotland. Prosperity seems to have mellowed the townsfolk to the extent that the Prince's arrival was generally welcomed and recriminations afterwards were few. Little or no damage was done to Derby, from whence a regiment of militia hastily raised by the Duke of Devonshire had fled in disorder the night before the Prince's arrival, taking the Whiggish element of the Corporation with them.

Yet change was already in train. In 1736 John Whitehurst F.R.S. (1713-88) came to the town from his native Congleton and set up as a most superior clockmaker, although by the 1750s his innovative genius had begun to embrace geology, scientific instruments, astronomy and numerous other topics. His acquaintanceship with James Ferguson brought him into contact with Benjamin Franklin, and the latter quickly carried him into the enlightened circle of Erasmus Darwin (who did not move from Lichfield to Derby until

4. A very early view of the Derwent from Exeter Bridge, looking north, taken in the 1850s by Richard Keene. The tower of All Saints' – the second highest in England – can be seen on the left, with a tannery on Full Street to its right, even then an old building. The spire belongs to St Alkmund's church, the tower near it to the Catholic church of St Mary (1838). To the right is the silk mill doubling shop (which collapsed in 1893) with the tower of the main silk mill (1717) beyond.

1782), Matthew Boulton and others who, in the next decade, came together to form the Lunar Society. Earlier, in 1717, the Derby silk mill had been founded by John and Thomas Lombe using technology hijacked in dramatic circumstances from the Piedmontese. This is generally thought to have been the first factory in England, with all the processes involved in spinning silk thread taking place under one roof with a common source of power – the waters of the Derwent.

In Derby, Whitehurst had attracted to his circle the painter Joseph Wright (1734-97), the Essex-born cartographer and engraver Peter Perez Burdett (1735-93), and the London-trained architect Joseph Pickford, who built long-vanished houses for both Whitehurst and Burdett as well as his extant *chef d'oeuvre*, St Helen's House, for the Whig grandee John Gisborne and a fascinating house for himself in Friar Gate, now a fine museum. At the same time, Jedidiah Strutt founded two mills in the town centre, one for silk goods, another for calico, the latter of a very advanced design, intended to be fireproof. In 1792 an Act was passed to release for development the remainder of a large tract of land straddling the western portion of Markeaton Brook, in order to raise money so that the improvement commissioners could pave and light the streets. A previous act (1768) had released another portion of this common along the north side of the development. The second act was fiercely disputed by some elements of the population, and with reason, for the availability of the brook as a power source led inevitably to the burgeoning of mills – mostly for silk and narrow tapes – and fairly squalid workers' housing which later became the nucleus of an unlovely area called the West End.

Jedidiah Strutt's son William (1756-1830), followed in the footsteps of Whitehurst (who went to London in the 1770s as H.M.'s Stamper of the Money Weights, where he wrote treatises on a bewildering variety of topics) as an innovator and polymath. In fact, many of William Strutt's innovations seemed to stem from ideas of Whitehurst, and one is inclined to suspect that Darwin passed them on to Strutt, his *protégé*. Darwin and Whitehurst had also been interested in founding an infirmary, and it was in 1806, after their deaths, that a bequest allowed Strutt to establish one using his own ideas (based on those put into effect by Whitehurst at St Thomas's, London, much earlier) for heating and ventilation. Thereafter, the Regency period saw much building, encouraged by the Improvement Commissioners and funded by private capital.

A man hardly connected with the potent circle of Whitehurst and Darwin was William Duesbury (1725-86) who around 1750 founded the China Factory on Nottingham Road with capital from a slightly suspect banker called Heath who also financed a pottery factory on Cockpit Hill at the same time. Only Duesbury's enterprise survived Heath's bankruptcy in 1779, an event which enabled the banker William Evans, a commissioner

5. A lithograph by the Victorian artist Moses Webster of the Derby China Factory, Nottingham Road, which was closed and demolished in 1848. The drawing was done from memory, many years later, but is the nearest we can get to its original appearance. One surviving architect's drawing of a weighbridge kiosk suggests that Pickford may have had a hand in its building.

in the bankruptcy, to acquire a mill in Darley Abbey. By 1782 he had turned it into a celebrated cotton mill, around which the miniscule hamlet of Darley Abbey was developed by his enlightened successors into a regency mill village, which mercifully survives almost intact.

In 1839, three newly-formed railway companies set up their headquarters and a combined station in Derby: the North Midland, Midland Counties and Birmingham & Derby Junction Railways. In 1844 they amalgamated to form the Midland Railway, which enterprise swiftly moved to establish works in Derby. In the wake of this, numerous foundries sprang up. Two foundries and an engineering concern – Jas. Fox & Sons., established under the patronage of Rev. Thomas Gisborne, Wright's friend – had however developed before the end of the 18th century, served by Outram's canal of 1796 which itself had replaced the Derwent Navigation of 1723-5.

Thus it was that in the first decades of the 19th century, Derby's population increased with alarming rapidity, and the girdle of estates round the town had to be breached in order for the future city to expand its housing stock. The streets in the town centre were still of medieval width, and the reformed municipality worked hard using private capital in the main to widen and improve them. A new generation of sound architects designed new houses and the improvements themselves were recorded for posterity by the early photographer Richard Keene (1825-94). He was the son of a mill manager and learned the skills of photography from the Rev. Edward Abney (father of Sir William, a photographic pioneer himself), a friend of Fox-Talbot, who had married a daughter of the Mundys of nearby Markeaton Hall, and was a frequent visitor there. Keene's earliest datable photograph was of Exeter House in 1854, but he was in business two years before. His luminous platinotypes recorded every change in the town's fabric over the next 40 years, and he also photographed the county gentry's seats during the same period – a most valuable record.

The era of foundries reached its culmination in 1907 when Rolls-Royce set up one on Nightingale Road, close to the larger of its mid-19th-century predecessors, to produce motor cars. Production was moved to Crewe in 1945 when the Derby facility had to be given over exclusively to the production of aero-engines. By this time, too, the Borough's boundaries had begun their relentless expansion, which culminated in the absorption of nearly all the peripheral villages by 1968. Before the Great War, the expansion of housing had necessitated the opening of tramways in 1880 (electrified in 1904), and a change had been made to trolleybuses in 1932, a mode of street transport phased out in 1967 in favour of motor 'buses.

Although an obvious strategic target for bombing in the Second World War, only two serious raids on Derby were at all effective, and most of the destruction wrought upon the historic fabric of the town was through the exigences of post-war planning. Today, the City of Derby is facing the problem of reconciling the need to attract tourists to its historic sites with the unprecedented boom in its economic fortunes which has resulted in many long-derelict sites vacated by the demolition of older, often historic, buildings being taken up for new development. Unfortunately, the quality of much of the new compares very unfavourably with the old, and equally unfavourably with that in other comparable towns. Yet despite this, Derby remains an extremely fine City with an historic tradition of national importance, and a pleasant, relaxed air produced by the timeless interaction of its friendly, welcoming citizens, and its fine historic core.

The Plates

Street Scenes

6. Queen Street in 1914 at the point where it curved around the west side of St Alkmund's church, with a range of charming 17th- and 18th-century buildings about to be demolished. The street on the right is the entrance to St Alkmund's Church Yard, Derby's only Georgian square, unhappily destroyed to make way for the Inner Ring Road in 1967.

7. A 1925 view south down the ancient spinal road, Queen Street, with the tower of All Saints' church (built 1511-32) rising like a cliff. The houses on the right were demolished in 1926 for street widening; those on the left survive. The timber-framed building is the *Old Dolphin Inn*, somewhat over-restored in the Edwardian period, and dating from the 17th century.

8. St Michael's Lane was the original route to Nottingham from the late Saxon *burh* of Derby, leaving Queen Street opposite Whitehurst's house and crossing the Derwent on a causeway, replaced by St Mary's Bridge in the 13th century. The building in the centre of the view, taken by Keene in the 1870s, is the first Wesleyan chapel of 1765. It was replaced in 1804 and became a workshop, being demolished, with the remainder of the area, in 1965. Not until 1989 did any new building begin on the site.

9. Walker Lane looking east to Queen Street. The lane was so named because of the presence of a walk mill or fulling mill in the vicinity in medieval times. The *Old Dolphin* can be seen on the right, and demolition for road widening had already begun in this 1926 view. The inn in the centre was the *Bull's Head*, demolished some years later to widen Full Street (to its left). The forest of chimneys in the background marks the grimy electricity power station of 1920, sited a road's width from the east end of All Saints' church, but mercifully removed in 1972.

10. The upper portion of Full Street between the *Old Dolphin* (left) and *Bull's Head* inns looking west towards Queen Street in *c*.1920. This part of Full Street was earlier known variously as Alderman Hill or Nanny Tag's Lane, and was widened in 1928 to accommodate the coke and fly-ash lorries which served the ghastly power station day and night.

11. Near All Saints' church, Queen Street becomes Irongate. Streets in Derby with the '-gate' suffix reflect a continuing use of Norse terminology during the early Middle Ages. Derby never in fact had walls or gates. This view by Keene, looking south down Irongate about 1857, shows two impressive buildings (left) swept away in 1866 for street widening: the oriel window of the jettied building must have been unique. The building to the right of the horse was refronted in 1693 as the *George*, one of the town's most celebrated coaching inns.

12. From Nanny Tag's Lane, Full Street turned south and ran parallel to Irongate beside the Derwent, turning into the Market Place in its north-east corner, shown here about 1921. Note the electric lamp standard with the Borough's arms (the Buck-in-the-Park) on its side. The house in the distance was built in 1723 for Alderman Samuel Heathcote, a notorious Jacobite.

13. Full Street photographed from the side of the Assembly Rooms, 1931. The house was built for the Jacobite Alderman Samuel Heathcote and was afterwards home to Dr. Erasmus Darwin, F.R.S., from 1782 to 1802. He had land on both sides of the Derwent, a riverside pavilion, a self-worked ferry controlled by ropes, and a mechanical well. Later, it was the town house of the Curzons of Breedon and more recently the local Conservative club: it was demolished in 1933, 211 years after it was built. Exeter House (demolished 1854) was reached through the gap to the right where the Police Station now stands.

14. The west side of Derby Market Place, looking north, photographed by Keene *c*.1857. On the left is the very grand house of Alderman Henry Franceys (d.1747), the town's leading apothecary. The buildings in the centre middle distance occupied the centre of the Market Place at this end; this part was known as Rotten Row, the north end was the Old Shambles, site of all the butchers' shops. The whole complex was demolished in 1870-77.

15.   Two exceptionally interesting views of Derby Market Place drawn in 1828 by G. Pickering (1779-1858). He was standing at the door to the old Assembly Rooms, the only building not shown. The upper view is looking west towards the Piazzas, erected for Samuel Crompton in 1708 (the east side of the complex which formed Rotten Row) with the 1731 Guildhall by Richard Jackson (demolished 1829) standing proud of the south side of the Market Place. The narrow street behind was called Breadleaps. The house at the extreme right was the *Virgin's Inn*, with the Duke of Newcastle's town house (late 16th-century, classicised *c.* 1685) extending over six bays two doors up. The lower view looks due south towards the Guildhall, with the clock John Whitehurst made in 1737 to become a burgess visible in the pediment. To its left is the Cornmarket, and the Piazzas are on the extreme right. The street running off in the centre is Tenant Street, with the *Royal Oak* inn to the right, which was replaced in 1890. In the distance on Tenant Street, the Shot Tower can be seen. The building to the left of the tower disguised Darby's Yard, behind which until about 1820 lay the Every family town house, a large 16th-century building. This area was demolished to allow for the building of Derwent Street over the new Exeter Bridge in 1850.

MARKET PLACE, DERBY.

16.   Derby Market Place looking north-east, *c*.1907. The Assembly Rooms are at the right, with Ramsden's restaurant adjoining. The *Virgin's Inn* has been replaced by Pountain & Co.'s wine merchants, and by T. H. Thorpe in 1893. The Newcastle House survived, unnoticed, until the entire north side was destroyed in 1971 to make way for the present Assembly Rooms. The statue is of Michael Thomas Bass M.P., erected 1884, and sculpted by Sir J. E. Boehm, Bt. Behind it are the Old Wine Vaults, affectionately known as 'The Sough'. Market stalls abound, naturally enough. They were banished in 1933.

17. Cornmarket ran south to the Markeaton Brook, widening *en route* to accommodate the marketing of grain. In this scene of around 1918 Victoria Street runs left to right, created in 1839 by culverting the Brook. The *Royal Hotel* on the right was built at the same time by Robert Wallace. The range of buildings behind the lamp standard was erected in 1910-11.

18. From the junction of Cornmarket and Victoria Street, the ancient trackway's route runs south along St Peter's Street, ascending the south bank of the old Brook. This view of lower St Peter's Street looks north, with Cornmarket in the distance. The photograph was taken by Richard Keene in 1856. Widening a decade and a half later accounted for all the buildings to the right. Messrs. George & George occupy the house of Joseph Strutt (1765-1844), originally a Restoration town house built for the Burtons of Aldercar Park. The building was replaced in 1878 by the present Midland Bank.

19.   Further up St Peter's Street, Babington Lane (named after the town house of the Babingtons of Dethick, long vanished) branched off to the south-west. Here, in the early 1920s, some sheep are being driven northwards, past the end of the lane. To the right the ancient route via Swarkestone Bridge divided from the London turnpike, taking the more direct route via Shardlow. This junction is for some unknown reason called The Spot.

20.   London Road, looking north-west towards The Spot, photographed *c.*1882. In the far distance are the buildings by J. Gascoyne, 1852, which replaced Babington Hall. On the right is the *Derwent Hotel*, built about 1840. None of these buildings on the east side of London Road have survived street widening. London Road was created as a turnpike road in 1758.

21. Running parallel with St Peter's Street, but alongside the littoral of the Derwent, was Tenant Street, which crosses the Markeaton Brook near where it enters the Derwent on Tenant Bridge, shown here in a photograph taken by Charles Keene in October 1931. The bridge parapet is visible between the cars on the left, but the brook is culverted to the right, becoming Albert Street (1846) which ran end-on to Victoria Street at St Peter's, or Gaol, Bridge. The continuation of Tenant Street is called The Morledge and runs up to Cockpit Hill (in the distance), once the site of Derby's short lived 12th-century castle. Note the base of the Shot Tower on the left – it was demolished the year after this photograph was taken.

22.   At the south end of The Morledge was Cockpit Hill. After the castle had vanished, the low mound of its motte was occupied by a cockpit. By October 1931, when Charles Keene took this view, most of it was covered by gently decaying 18th-century artisans' housing. The small open area was usually given over to stallholders, with the *Canal Tavern* (right) to provide refreshment. All this was demolished in 1972 to make way for the Eagle Centre, an ugly and environmentally disastrous shopping precinct.

23.   Green Lane, the original route to Burton-upon-Trent, rose southwards from the southern loop of the Brook. This 1914 view looks north, All Saints' tower being just visible through the heat haze in the distance. The building in the foreground on the left is the Hippodrome, opened the previous year, and designed by Alexander MacPherson of Derby. Beyond it is Macklin Street. The wall on the right hides The Hollies, the elegant Regency residence of Dr. George Sims, demolished in 1925.

24.   The Wardwick, looking south-east from St Werburgh's church towards Victoria Street. Still one of the finest streets in the city, it is seen here in 1906, unwidened, with interlaced tram tracks. The building on the left was constructed in 1780 for Dr. Francis Fox, but destroyed by street widening in 1913. Set back is the Museum (1879), and visible beyond is the Mechanics' Institute,   as rebuilt in 1882 by Arthur Coke-Hill (1847-1907) and G. H. Sheffield (1844-82). The 17th-century house with gables is the surviving portion of the Jacobean House of 1611, long occupied by the Gisbornes, but semi-demolished to accommodate Becket Street in 1852, its park later infilled.

25.   From The Wardwick one travels west into Friar Gate, which continues west. As this street approached Ashbourne Road it widened to accommodate the beast market, with an open space on its northern edge called Nuns' Green. This was developed in 1768-78 with elegant houses, seen on the left of this 1909 picture. The exception is the graceful pedimented range, erected by Joseph Cooper of Derby in 1841 on the site of William Hiorn's 1756 County Gaol. The large building just visible behind the trees on the right was R. Ernest Ryley's Deaf and Dumb Institution of 1893, demolished in 1973.

26.   Beyond St Alkmund's church, the ancient route north was diverted by the laying out of Darley Park in the 18th century to form Duffield Road, pictured here at the turn of the century. By this date, the street was lined with opulent villas ranging in date from *c.*1840 to Edwardian. The chain link railing was installed in 1881, and was recently restored.

27.   A boundary extension in 1928 and the acquisition by the Borough, partly by bequest, in the following year of Markeaton Hall and its 100-acre park, landscaped by William Emes of nearby Bowbridge Fields, enabled the town to build its Ring Road. It is seen here looking south-west when new in 1930, at the point where it crossed the Kedleston Road and bisected the parkland. It was drastically widened and rebuilt in 1980.

Churches and Chapels

28.   A 1901 view up Bridge Gate, looking west, with Henry Isaac Stevens' St Alkmund's church of 1843 looming above the heads of passers by. This was the site of the ancient minster church which pre-dated the founding of the Saxon *burh*. The road probably followed the line of the ancient town ditch, *c.*1250, when the bridge was built. The jettied building on the left, on the corner of Darley Lane, was latterly a confectioner's shop, and was of 15th-century date. On the right are Wilmot's Almohouses ('the Black Hospital'), rebuilt in 1834 and demolished in 1936. The remainder of the buildings were destroyed in 1966, along with St Alkmund's Church Yard, Derby's only Georgian square, for the Inner Ring Road.

29. The other pre-Danish church in the area later to become Derby is St Werburgh's. Its proximity to the Markeaton Brook led over the centuries to repeated subsidence, the tower being replaced in 1610, and the body of the church in 1699 and again in 1894. In this view by Keene of *c.*1860, the 1610 tower can be seen with the delightful baroque nave, toplit by a dome. Inside, where Samuel Johnson married Tetty Porter in 1735, was a wrought-iron font cover by Robert Bakewell, a fine monument to the Whinyates family by Sir Francis Chantrey and a superb carved oak reredos. The present nave was designed by Sir Arthur Blomfield; all the other buildings in view, including the *Buck-in-the-Park Inn* (left), survive today, although the church is now redundant, and is in the process of being converted into a shopping precinct.

30. All Saints' was the second minster church, founded early in the 10th century. In 1927 it became the Cathedral of the newly-created diocese of Derby. The medieval church, in a state of serious disrepair, was demolished almost overnight in 1723. James Gibbs designed the new church and Francis Smith of Warwick built it, retaining the old and magnificent tower. John Whitehurst rebuilt the clock and Sorocold's carillon in 1745. The photograph was taken by Keene from his house in Irongate shortly after street widening had reduced the church yard at the west end in 1873.

31.   The interior of All Saints' is a superb tribute to the quality of craftsmanship in Derby in the early 18th century. Robert Bakewell's wrought iron screen can be seen in this Edwardian view of a Mayoral inauguration service. The photograph was taken from the splendid oak gallery carved by Thomas Trimmer, and there are monuments by John Smithson (to Bess of Hardwick), Roubiliac, Ruysbrack, Nollekens, Westmacott, Chantrey, Joseph Pickford, George Moneypenny and Richard Brown, a talented local man. In 1969-72 the Venetian window was taken down and a retro-choir, song school and vestry were added, to the designs of Sir Ninian and Sebastian Comper.

32. Another church of ancient foundation which was probably absorbed by the town before Domesday is St Peter's, Derby's only town church to retain its medieval appearance, despite two Victorian rebuildings, the first by G.E. Street in 1859. The photograph, again by Richard Keene, shows it in the 1860s, before the tower was rebuilt. The gabled building, left, is the Derby School, founded under a charter of Queen Mary I in 1555. It was not vacated in favour of St Helen's House until 1861, but the school is due finally to lose its identity in 1989. The old grammar school building is now a photographer's studio. The railings were, apparently, provided by a Mr. Hunt in 1840, but were replaced during road widening in 1876.

33. St Michael's church was one of the smaller town churches extant from at least the 11th century and grouped along the ancient north-south route. The medieval church collapsed in 1856, and its replacement by H. I. Stevens is depicted here, c.1927. It, too, was made redundant at the end of the 1970s, and was imaginatively converted into architects' offices by Derek Latham in 1985. This view from the top of Walker Lane, cleared in advance for street widening, shows part of Balguy's House, behind the church, demolished in 1962.

34.   The medieval bridge over the Derwent probably always had its own chapel from the time of its construction in the 13th century, but the surviving chapel of St Mary-on-the-Bridge dates from the 15th century and later. After the Dissolution, it had a chequered history, becoming a Presbyterian meeting house after the Restoration, later a workshop (with a handsome gabled house of 1700 attached) and was restored as a chapel by the Derbyshire Archaeological Society with money from the Haslam family in 1930. Beyond it, in this 1860s' view, is a boiler works; today, the Inner Ring Road passes by on a concrete causeway, only ten feet from the ancient fabric of the chapel.

35.   In the more constructive climate of William and Mary, the Presbyterians were able to leave the Bridge chapel, and build anew in Friar Gate. Shown here is the chapel they erected in 1698, but with a Victorian tripartite porch. The interior was very fine, galleried, and with a ceiling supported by four giant Tuscan columns. In 1782 the Presbyterians sold it to the Unitarians (the Strutts paying the bill), and they were bought out by Viking Properties in the early 1970s who replaced the chapel, and the County Club to its right, with a huge, unlovely office block. The gate-piers to the left are by Joseph Pickford for The Friary, Samuel Crompton's elegant and surviving town house; the now vanished gates are by Benjamin Yates. Photograph *c*.1895.

36.   Having left their chapel in Friar Gate, the Presbyterians opened a new one on Brookside, later Victoria Street, in 1782, built in a debased Palladian style. In 1836, increased numbers caused them to rebuild, their architect William Mansfield Cooper (son of Joseph) producing a most harmonious neo-Grecque building which, however, had to be replaced again less than thirty years later when the Nottingham architect Thomas Chambers Hine (1813-99) built them a much larger edifice in gothic style. This in its turn lasted barely a century, succumbing to Messrs. Ranby's redevelopment in 1962. The W. M. Cooper building is here shown in a lithograph of the 1840s.

37. The rapid expansion of mills and accompanying housing north of Friar Gate from 1792 led to the provision of a new Anglican church – St John's, Bridge Street. This, the work of Francis Goodwin (1784-1835), was built in 1826-8 as a miniature version of the chapel of King's, Cambridge, and incorporated much cast iron: fittings, tracery and decoration from the Derby foundry of Messrs. Weatherhead, Glover & Co. of Duke Street. A large school was provided next to the church (left). Before the end of the century, the cupolas were found to be unsafe and were removed from the towers which rather spoiled its appearance. Mercifully, this church still serves its original purpose.

38. Shortly after the building of St John's, Bridge Street, another new church was erected on the south of the town, on the Normanton Road, near the summit of Green Lane. This, shown here c.1876, was Christ Church, built in 1835 by Matthew Habershon (1789-1852); the rear of the vicarage can be seen to the right. It is today used by a Serbian Orthodox community.

39. The Catholics had built their first place of worship since the Reformation in Chapel Street in 1813, but in 1838-44 replaced it by a spectacular gothic church on Bridge Gate, dedicated to St Mary, by A. W. N. Pugin (1811-52) aided by a substantial grant from the 16th Earl of Shrewsbury. This photograph, taken in 1934, shows part of the chancel, with a wrought-iron screen by John Hardman of London. The church was restored in 1988-89, although liturgical adventurism has caused some of the wrought iron to be removed.

40. Pugin also designed a presbytery (now demolished) and, on the site of Duesbury's former China Factory, an ambitious convent dedicated to St Vincent de Paul, 1841-43. Unfortunately it proved to be too ambitious and was demolished in 1863. The sisters moved into a pair of Georgian houses on the west side of St Mary's (where they still flourish), and the site was redeveloped. Two gothic external wall entrances were saved, one going to the *Corporation Hotel*, Cattle Market, the other to a house on Radbourne Street; both have since vanished. The iron railings went to Stevens' Diocesan Training College, but were taken away in World War Two.

41. In 1804 the Methodists abandoned their original chapel in St Michael's Lane (*see* plate 8) and established a new chapel on the corner of King Street and Chapel Street. This was again rebuilt in 1841 to a most dignified neo-Grecque design by James Simpson of Leeds, but was demolished at the beginning of the 1960s to make room for a multi-storey car park. The view is from an Edwardian postcard.

42. Another highly distinguished design was that by Henry Isaac Stevens for the Congregationalists, on the north-eastern corner of London Road and Traffic Street, built in 1845-6. Stevens is chiefly remembered for a varied series of gothic churches, yet his classical buildings, although fewer, are amongst the most satisfying. The need to widen Traffic Street as part of the Inner Ring Road scheme necessitated the destruction of this building in 1962, although it had been converted rather adventurously into a cinema in 1934 by T. H. Thorpe and Partners. This photograph was taken by Hurst & Wallace, c.1890.

43. Hand-in-hand with the expansion of the Borough's population and the provision of places of worship came a need for burial space. This view of the monument to Rev. John Gregory Deodatus Pike (1784-1854), father of the Baptist movement in Derby, was taken by Keene in the latter year. It stands in the new cemetery in the Uttoxeter New Road, laid out in 1843. The designer and sculptor was a talented artist from South Wingfield, James Barlow Robinson (1821-83). He had served his apprenticeship on the Palace of Westminster and had a wide country house practice, as well as having his home and works at No. 11, Uttoxeter New Road – convenient for the major local source of his work.

Public Buildings

44.   One of Derby's oldest public buildings had been the first bridge across the Derwent (*c*.1250), with its Chapel of St Mary (*see* plate 34). This view of about 1935 shows the bridge's successor, promoted by William Strutt (whose obituary claims he designed it). It was, however, actually designed by Thomas Harrison of Chester and built by James Trubshawe the elder of Great Heywood, 1789-94. Beyond can be seen the Bridge Chapel (one of only five still extant in England) as restored in 1930, with the Bridge Chapel House beyond, where Alderman Thomas Eaton's windows were twice smashed by Reform rioters in 1831. The Ring Road closes the view to the left today, the vast concrete Causey Bridge blocking off the view south down this attractive reach of the river.

45. The medieval Guildhall in the Market Place survived as a store and lock-up until 1730, but had outlived its usefulness by the early 17th century, if not before. Accordingly, civic functions moved to the Moot Hall, on the east side of Irongate. The building is seen here in a 19th-century watercolour viewed north-west up the yard behind the *Virgin's Inn*, although the entrance was once from a wide courtyard off Irongate. It was a tall, multi-gabled brick building with stone dressings and, although it lost its formal civic functions in 1732 and its social ones in 1764, it has survived as a five-storey office block of the Derbyshire Building Society. It can still be identified, immured behind the new Assembly Rooms, and forgotten by most.

46. In a sense the Borough's wells might be considered as public buildings. Some, like the elegant cupola which covered the Conduit in the Market Place, were highly significant. Most became redundant after Sorocold had established the town's water supply in 1693; the remainder vanished when the waterworks were established in 1849. The sole survivor was Becket Well (deriving from the medieval word *bouget* = bucket, and not from St Thomas of Canterbury, as was once thought) just south of Victoria Street. This had a well-head dated to the 1640s, but the distinctive conical superstructure, perhaps inspired by the pyramid of Cestius, Rome, was probably Sorocold's work. It was swept away in 1963-4 to make way for a multi-storey car park surrounded by a small, ugly shopping precinct.

47.   The finest surviving public building in Derby is the Shire Hall, built in 1659-60 to designs by George Eaton. Later, in 1772, it was enlarged by Joseph Pickford, and then vastly expanded by Matthew Habershon to become the County Court in the 1820s. In this early 20th-century view the Assize procession has come to rest in the *cour-d'honneur*, flanked by the police escort, the pikemen and the trumpeters. The last Assize Judge stayed in the Judge's Lodgings (1811), on the right, in 1971. Thereafter, the building continued as a crown court until 1989, but then closed, its future uncertain.

48.   Most public buildings in the 18th century were erected as a result of public subscriptions or private munificence. The Piazzas were built in 1708 in the Market Place, on the east side of the block which formed Rotten Row and housed the Shambles, or Butchery. The idea was to provide sheltered shopping below and workshops above, but the donor, Samuel Crompton I, an opulent banker, found that lettings were slow and the upper space was mainly given over to storage. In 1871 the Shambles and the northern part were demolished, the rest following when further finance had been raised, in 1877. Keene's photograph was taken in 1871 when demolition was well advanced.

49. There were several groups of almshouses in Derby. Among the most handsome were those built under a bequest from Alderman Large, of 1713, for the widows of clergymen. They stood on the south side of Friar Gate, and are shown here, *c.*1865, in a photograph by Richard Keene, before the street was planted with London planes in 1869-70. The building was replaced in 1880 by more commodious almshouses, which still stand, although now offices.

50. Each parish had a workhouse, most being built or upgraded in the 18th century, as with the All Saints' workhouse in Walker Lane which was built to the designs of William Trimmer in 1729. This became redundant a century later, but survived as workshops until demolished in 1925 to make way for C. H. Aslin's new Queen Street Baths. It is shown here, photographed by Borough Surveyor, C. B. Sherwin, during demolition.

51. Up until 1764, Derby supported a Borough Assembly (in the Moot Hall) and a County Assembly (in Full Street). In 1762, a committee of noblemen and gentlemen raised subscriptions for the building of new, combined Assembly Rooms. These were designed by Washington Shirley, 5th Earl Ferrers, and built by Joseph Pickford, much of whose architectural vocabulary is discernible in the detailing. Ramsden's, to the right, was built shortly afterwards as a catering establishment to produce suppers for the Assemblies. This photograph was taken in 1927.

52. It took another nine years of fund-raising before the interior of the Assembly Rooms could be decorated and fitted out. This was done in 1773 by Abraham Denstone of Derby to designs prepared by Robert Adam; the result was very fine indeed, comparable to anything in England. Yet, after a minor fire in February 1963, the Council took the opportunity to demolish all but the façade, in furtherance of its plans to build hideous new civic halls on the north side of the Market Place. The façade, originally to be incorporated, was eventually given to the Crich Tramway Museum in 1972.

53. The Derbyshire General Infirmary was built on London Road to the designs of Samuel Brown and William Strutt, 1806-10. A terracotta statue of Aesculapius by William Coffee graced the roof. The heating and ventilation system, by Strutt and Charles Sylvester and evolved from Whitehurst's ideas, had a fatal flaw: there was no means of cleaning the ducts, and the building had to be rebuilt by H. I. Stevens in the 1860s (advised by Florence Nightingale). But ultimately it all had to be replaced with a pavilion-style hospital by Young & Hall, 1891-6. The photograph, by Richard Keene, was taken c.1860.

54. William Hiorn's County Gaol of 1756 in Friar Gate had become inadequate by the 1820s, and an advanced new one was built nearby to designs by Francis Goodwin in 1826-7, at the end of Vernon Street, laid out by Goodwin from Friar Gate. This was terminated by a most impressive Doric façade, which survived when the gaol buildings were demolished in 1927-8. This view was taken on 22 July 1932, when the site was being prepared to make a dog-racing track. The surviving façade can be seen from within the brick curtain walls, studded by 'Martello towers' put in by John Mason of Derby in 1831 after the Reform Rioters nearly succeeded in storming the building. In 1988 greyhounds competed in their last race and the following year planning consent was obtained for flats and offices.

55. In the 1820s, the Corporation bought up houses on the south side of the Market Place and replaced the 1731 Guildhall with a new one, set back, which freed more space in the Market Place. This, shown here in a lithograph of 1830, was built to designs by Matthew Habershon in 1829. Whitehurst's turret clock was transferred to the new building but, along with most of the Borough records, was destroyed by fire in 1841.

56. The next Guildhall utilised the ground floor and end bays of the destroyed building, and was designed by Henry Duesbury (d.1872), a London architect descended from the founder of the Derby China Factory. The bas-reliefs were sculpted by John Bell (1812-96). This view by Hurst & Wallace, c.1890, shows the pleasant range of buildings flanking the Guildhall; all survive except Smith's clocks (extreme right) and the two adjacent, replaced in 1974 by a glass and granite bank, mercifully built to scale. Note the ubiquitous cabbies' rest, and the line of cabs to the right of it. One of these structures survived until 1984 as a snack bar in Albert Street.

57.   Another extremely fine Greek revival building was the 1836 Mechanics' Institute, which replaced a grand 17th-century house which had become a slum, in The Wardwick. The Institute was promoted by Joseph Strutt, Francis Fox and other Whig philanthropists. The lecture hall, seen here in a lithograph, acting as a temporary museum for the Derby Philosophical Society, was an extremely handsome room. The façade was demolished in 1880 to widen the street. W. M. Cooper's original building is today difficult to discern, as the great lecture hall is subdivided into shops, and the Strand front is stuccoed with meaningless embellishments designed by G. H. Sheffield and Arthur Hill in 1882, who also rebuilt the Wardwick front.

58.   The culverting of the Markeaton Brook enabled a consortium to redevelop the north side. The *Royal Hotel*, on the corner with Cornmarket, and the Athenaeum Club, fronting Victoria Street, were designed by Robert Wallace and built in 1839. The Athenaeum Club originally sported a frieze by John Henning the elder (1771-1851) of the Panathenaic procession – just visible above the first-floor windows between the projecting bays. Beyond is T. C. Hine's Presbyterian chapel which replaced that illustrated in plate 36. In the foreground, the road rises over the arch of William Strutt's St Peter's Bridge of 1787, still partly in existence beneath the tarmac. The glorious Five Lamps, cast by Messrs. Weatherhead, Glover & Co. in 1839, stands beyond, at the head of Cornmarket. It was removed to the junction of Kedleston and Duffield roads about 1905 to open the top of Cornmarket to traffic. The photograph is by W. W. Winter, *c.*1890.

59. In 1852 the Bishop of Lichfield, John Lonsdale, founded a training college for women teachers on the Uttoxeter New Road, opposite the cemetery. It was designed by H. I. Stevens, and was set in three acres of pleasant grounds. It was extended twice and the chapel was added by P. H. Currey (1865-1942) early in the present century. The college is now the Derbyshire College of Higher Education, but it abandoned these buildings in 1985, hoping to make a killing by demolishing them and building bijou housing on the site. The Civic Society, however, managed to get it spot-listed, and it has now found a new use, though the grounds, regrettably, are nonetheless being built over.

60. The Grand Theatre was Derby's second, the 1773 theatre on Bold Lane having been converted into a Gospel Hall by the killjoy Alderman Wilkins in 1864. It was designed by Oliver Essex and built in 1886 on Babington Lane. This photograph was taken from Gower Street. Council offices (by George Thompson c.1870) can be seen on the left, and the retaining wall of the grounds of Abbott's Hill House is to the right. The street was anciently called Blood Lane. The theatre survives, although now a night club.

61. In 1840 Joseph Strutt (1765-1844), brother of William, presented a public park, the Arboretum, to his fellow-townsmen. This consisted of 11 acres, landscaped by John Claudius Loudon (1783-1843), lying on the west side of the Osmaston Road – the ancient route south from the town. The main entrance, shown here, was designed by Henry Duesbury. Today it is a roofless shell and the Arboretum itself is only just beginning to recover from 70 years of unforgivable neglect, in spite of the fact that this was arguably the first municipal park in England. Photograph by Keene, c.1858.

62. Until 1869-70, Victoria Street ended at the intersection shown in this view of 1879, where ancient St James's Bridge carried St James's Lane to join the east end of The Wardwick. The building on the left is the dignified General Post Office, by J. Williams of London, 1869; those beyond are by Giles & Brookhouse, built five years later to line the Strand, a street created by further culverting of the brook at the expense of Alderman Sir Abraham Woodiwiss, Mayor 1880-81, an opulent railway contractor.

63. In about 1825 Joseph Hall, a spar manufacturer, established public baths in St Helen's Walk; in 1852, H. I. Stevens built the first municipal baths in Full Street. This 1904 photograph shows the second municipal baths, designed by John Ward and built on Reginald Street near the Arboretum, shortly after opening. They were closed with hardly a murmur in 1983 and only the façade survives, the Moorish-style Turkish Baths and other delights behind having been sacrificed to housing development.

64. Ashbourne Road from the mouth of Shaw Street showing Ashgate School, designed by Thomas Coulthurst and John Soames Storey and opened in March 1880, shortly before this photograph was taken by Keene. The passing of the 1870 Education Act was the signal for a burst of school building by the Borough (County Borough from 1889) Council. Coulthurst & Storey built a good many schools, but this was one of their grandest. It still stands, although the tower has been reduced.

65. By the end of the First World War, Derby badly needed a second grammar school. The Bemrose family, opulent printers for over a century, made this possible with financial assistance. Alexander MacPherson designed the new Bemrose School on Uttoxeter Road, shown here shortly after completion in 1930. It became comprehensive in the early 1970s, but is otherwise little altered.

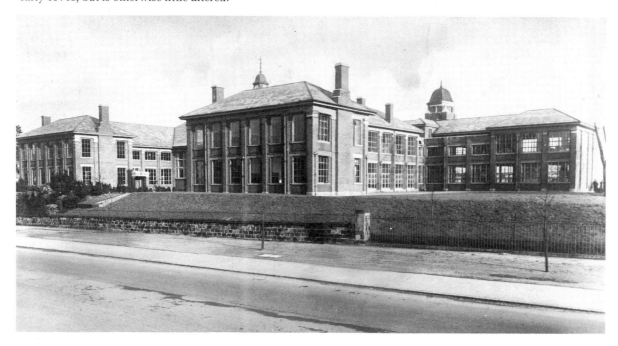

Shops

66.   Interior of Messrs. Cope & Taylor, apothecaries, photographed by W. W. Winter in 1935. The business had been started by the Franceys family in the 17th century, and after the death of Alderman Henry Franceys (the only tradesman allowed into the old County Assembly) during his Mayoralty in 1747, it passed through many hands, surviving almost unchanged until 1971, although no doubt the bravura display of sponges had been superseded! The grand 1690s' building has survived and the shopfittings of *c.*1860 are at the Museum, although not yet on display.

67. Ashbourne Road at the junction with Brick Street and Uttoxeter Old Road in the early 1920s. The delightful group of buildings, ranging from late medieval to early 18th century, has been known for very many years as Goodall's Corner, after the shop on the left, a pork butcher, established since the early 1880s. The whole ensemble is still, mercifully, intact.

68. The lower end of Sadler Gate photographed in about 1920. The decaying 16th-century range, housing a tripe dresser and a miniscule confectioner's, has since been re-fronted. Most of the buildings in this street are of similar date with Georgian or later façades. The Old Derby Dining Rooms of J. H. Bullock claim to have been established 130 years, although research so far has failed to establish the veracity of this! Mason's, an old established paint firm, still in business, occupied the shop on the right.

69.   On the other side of Sadler Gate, opposite the Strand Arcade (just to the left of the view shown in plate 68), is today the only surviving 16th-/early 17th-century front. It is seen in this photograph of *c.*1880 jointly occupied by Mark Goodwin, 'practical haircutter', and Joseph Eagers' cutlery emporium. Note the elaborate gas lampion to the left. Derby's first gas light was set up outside the Guildhall in 1820, the date of the building of the gas works between Bold Lane and Friar Gate.

70. Sadler Gate Bridge, viewed in about 1920. Although the Markeaton Brook had been culverted in 1870 it still ran beneath the road in front of the shops, and the bridge remains *in situ* lying between the lady with the shopping basket and the camera. The buildings, including J. T. Foster's (a saddler) and Freeborough's delightful early 18th-century edifice, were demolished *c.*1950 to make way for a garage, now an unlovely supermarket. Although the bridge has been unseen for almost 120 years, a street name plate still proclaims its existence.

71. West side of Rotten Row, Market Place, in 1877, just after the east side had been demolished. The building on the left was Wm. Richardson's, tailor, next to Smith's bank, closed and ready for demolition to make way for a new bank designed by Thomas Isborne of London, which has survived. The narrow but engaging Italianate building has also survived, albeit with a rebuilt roofline. *Mason's Tap House Inn* had closed by 1903 after at least 80 years' existence. Its last proprietor, William Selvey, optimistically renamed it the *Criterion Vaults*.

72. St Peter's Street, west side, in 1875. The shops were, from the right, Alderman Wilkins's printing and bookselling emporium, R. & J. Dick's boot and shoe manufactory, Jennings & Sons, clothiers, Alf Clark, hairdresser, and Samuel Bloor, saddler (on the corner of St Peter's Church Yard). The shop beyond the church was James Shackleton's, a late medieval building soon to be demolished. Its superb carved dragon post is now in Derby Museum. C. J. Shackleton, the son, was for many years the flamboyant serjeant-at-mace of the corporation.

73. An historic landmark disappearing in 1922. Edward Clulow's bookshop (the business still flourishes) had been built in 1869-71 for J. & G. Haywood, ironmongers and founders, to the design of George Thompson (1803-82), but its chief glory was Owen Jones's cast-iron façade, made by Haywood's in their own works. The site, at the lower east part of Irongate, became part of Messrs. Barlow and Taylor's department store, now the Derbyshire Building Society.

74. New Normanton was a spreading suburb consisting mainly of brick terraced housing between the ancient village of Normanton and the southern boundary of the town, built to house the Borough's burgeoning workforce. At the south end of New Normanton, two major arteries through the suburb converged at a grandiose public house called *The Cavendish*, opposite which, in 1910, the Derby Co-operative Society (founded in 1850) built a large shop, shown here in about 1914. It housed a grocery, butchery and, more unusually, a creamery, with a 400-seat meeting hall above. It dwarfed the four small shops beyond, running up Stenson Road to the corner of Vincent Street.

Houses and Homes

75.   The earliest large house which survived into the 20th century was the prosaically but misleadingly named Old Mayor's Parlour. Lying on a curving burgage plot on the east side of Tenant Street, this large, five-gabled timber-framed house of 1489 (probably built as a town house for a county grandee) survived until the then Borough Council demolished it in 1948, after pledging its future security to the chairman of the Derbyshire Archaeological Society. Its east front had been rebuilt in about 1665, after the house had been divided by Dr. Percival Willoughby (1596-1685), the pioneer gynaecologist. The site then became a bus park, and is now to house a computer-designed hotel.

76.   Newcastle House, on the north side of the Market Place, in the 1950s. This began life in the second half of the 16th century as a large brick edifice connected with the Talbot family; there was a 15th-century house embedded in the rear. It was classicised around 1675-80 by the Dukes of Newcastle, the first Duke (as Earl) having entertained Charles I here in 1637. It was demolished, with the remainder of the row, in 1971-2 without any protest. Only a part of the exuberant Restoration plaster ceiling from the Great Room on the first floor was saved and built into the Assembly Rooms which replaced it.

77.   The Jacobean House was built in 1611 and truncated in 1852 for the building of Becket Street, beyond the wall on the left in this view of *c*.1865. Alderman Francis Jessopp had previously had a two-acre park through which ran the Bramble Brook, a tributary of the Markeaton Brook. It was he who built the gothic stable block, right, and had architect John Price record the original house in plan and elevation before it was reduced. The park is now occupied by a government building; the house is an estate agents'.

78. On the corner of Sadler Gate and Irongate stands Lloyd's Bank, built by Alderman Joshua Smith at the beginning of the 18th century. Only the ground floor has been rebuilt; its previous owner had been William Bemrose, the printer, who set up there in the early years of the 19th century. The four-bay building to the right was the new front added to the ancient *George Inn* – one of Derby's historic coaching inns – in 1693 by Alderman Samuel Heathcote the elder. The part visible in this 1921 photograph was by then divided between the *Globe Inn* (now the *Mister Jorrocks*) and Foulds' Music Shop, still flourishing on the site.

79. The second decade of the 18th century saw the building of a tall town house to the north of Babington Lane by the antiquary Dr. Simon Degge (1694-1729). It is seen here in 1925 with its late 19th-century service wing and carriage entrance, from Babington Lane in 1925, the year before it was demolished and replaced by shops. It had been built in the park of the town house of the Catholic martyr Anthony Babington of Dethick, which stood lower down the street until about 1811. The park wall of the 18th-century house can be seen resting on that of its predecessor.

80.   The grandest house in St Mary's Gate, the still-elegant street which runs westward from the Cathedral tower, was St Mary's Gate House, built in 1724-5 for merchant and landowner William Osborne, perhaps to a design by James Gibbs. The ironwork on the perron was by Bakewell (as were the main gates, now gracing the Cathedral) and is now, with the roof urns, at Barton Blount Hall. The house was adapted by Fenton of Chelmsford as a Baptist chapel in the 1840s, and was demolished by Messrs. Kennings in 1938, who have since utilised the site as a car park.

81.   Devonshire House, Cornmarket, was built for the Duke of Devonshire in 1750 and used sporadically until the first decade of the 19th century when the Dukes switched to the newly-built Judges' Lodgings in St Mary's Gate to escape the increasing insalubrity of the Cornmarket area. After that, the once grand town house was divided as shops and offices. In 1969 the five bays nearest the camera were tragically demolished in order to build a concrete and windowless Littlewood's store. Since then Ramsden's, formerly caterers to the old Assembly Rooms, has closed, and Sainsbury's has moved away. This photograph was taken in 1939.

82. The grandest surviving house in Derby, and arguably the city's finest building, is St Helen's House, built by Joseph Pickford in 1767 for the Whig grandee John Gisborne of Yoxall Lodge, Staffordshire. It was sold by his son, Rev. Thomas Gisborne, to William Strutt, F.R.S., who made many innovative domestic improvements. His son, 1st Lord Belper, sold it to Derby School which added an ugly wing in a pastiche style (in the centre of this photograph behind Sir Reginald Blomfield's war memorial of 1923) and a pleasant chapel of 1894 by Percy Heylin Currey (1865-1942), an old boy. This 1941 view shows the widened King Street. Road widening destroyed Pickford's neo-classical screen wall and most of the semi-circular walled courtyard behind.

83. St Helen's House: the hall. The house was built on a variation of the villa plan, to facilitate entertaining. George Moneypenny carved the fire places; Benjamin Yates (d.1778) made the wrought-iron balustrade on the stairs, virtually identical to those he made for Staunton Harold Hall for Lord Ferrers, and Abraham Denstone (1723-79) executed the stucco work. The photograph shows the alterations made by the school, and was taken by Winter in 1936. The school moved out in the late 1960s, and this magnificent building now faces an uncertain future.

84.   Until the Reformation Little Chester boasted seven prebendal farms, each of which supported one of the canons of the College of All Saints. Since the unpardonable demolition in 1964 of Little Chester Manor House (found recently to have been built directly on to Roman foundations) only two survive. In this photograph of Stone House Prebend, formerly 'Le Subdeene's Farm', part of the medieval fabric can be discerned overlaid by subsequent phases to the 18th century. The house also boasts a Jacobean panelled room and fine overmantel.

85.   Many houses in Derby were built at right angles to the road, their orientation dictated by the narrow burgess plots laid out when the Saxon *burh* was founded. This house, of early 17th-century date, was once quite substantial, with its brick string courses and shaped gables. By the time it was revealed for the camera by demolition in advance of the building of Queen Street Baths in 1927, it had become a reeking tenement in Tiger Yard behind the inn of that name. It was demolished soon afterwards, but others survive in Sadler Gate.

86. Rear of shops on the north-west side of Sadler Gate seen from Palfree's Yard in the second decade of the 20th century. These buildings have been refronted so this rear view is an important indication of their true age. Palfree's Yard was named after Samuel Palfree, a farrier who lived and worked there for a long time. He was succeeded by his daughter, a veterinary practitioner. On her retirement in 1979, the Yard was refurbished as a highly unsuccessful shopping precinct called Old Blacksmith's Yard, the centrepiece of which is the reconstituted remains of the 15th-century house found behind Newcastle House in 1971 (*see* plate 76).

87. Before the Evans family built the Boar's Head Cotton Mill at Darley Hall, one of the few residences within the parish was Folly House on the east side of the Derwent, a 17th-century farm house, later made to appear Georgian. It is seen here in the early part of the present century, complete with footbridge to its front door. Today the house has been reduced, losing the gable to the right. As a result, much of its charm is lost.

88. (*above left*) Many once elegant early buildings stand unrecognised in the most unlikely parts of Derby. This early 18th-century house in Green Lane, opposite the end of Gower Street, was photographed in the early 1920s. Although Holloway's curio shop has long gone, the building survives, though ruined by later shopfronting and unsuitable fenestration. This may have been the site of the Academy run by the science-minded father of the philosopher Herbert Spencer.

89. (*above*) Friar Gate, between St Werburgh's church and Ford Street, where Nuns' Green once began, contains buildings going back to the 17th century, like the much-altered gabled building shown in this photograph taken about 1918. The brick house is early 18th-century. Both survive, but have been marred by subsequent shopfronting. Simpson's Printing Works, left, is a fine Regency house, gutted behind the façade in 1925 but, like the others, still extant. All would have been built for the prosperous tradesmen or attorneys. The public house on the extreme right is the *Rising Sun*.

90. (*left*) Two very interesting houses, both demolished in the 1930s, in the once fashionable Full Street. The gabled building was long the home of the Peach family, later of Kirk Langley; that on the left was built between 1765 and 1768 as an essay in gothick by Joseph Pickford for his friend, the cartographer, engraver and pioneer aquatinter, Peter Perez Burdett (1735-93). By the time of the photograph, c.1912, it had become the All Saints' Institute. This part of Full Street, directly behind the church, was known as All Saints' Church Yard in the 18th century. Only the southerly part of the street then bore its familiar name.

91. Herbert Spencer (1820-1903) was one of the most important philosophers of the 19th century, and he was born at 37, Exeter Place, shown here in a photograph taken in the earlier part of the present century. Spencer *père* was the headmaster of a modest private academy in Green Lane (*see* plate 88) and his house, built *c.*1815, is typical of the sort of terraced housing built for lesser professional men and shopkeepers. This street was carelessly swept away in the early 1960s to make way for the Inner Ring Road.

92. London Terrace, London Road, on the other hand, was intended for the middle ranks of the professional classes when built to the designs of H. I. Stevens in 1840. The Terrace is shown here in a photograph by Keene of *c.*1862. St George's church was built speculatively by G. Botham in 1832. It was replaced in 1904 by Holy Trinity, which survives. In the distance is Stevens' Congregational chapel (*see* plate 42).

93. Increasingly in the earlier 19th century, professional men and manufacturers wanted to live in suburban villas. This view is a perspective by the architect Benjamin Wilson of Sheffield and Derby of Stanley House, built in 1851 for Thomas Swingler, ironfounder. It survives, much extended (in 1882 and 1976), as an old peoples' home, on Duffield Road. Beyond is a modest later Regency villa by the brothers Cooper, The Mount.

94. A tramcar descends Dairyhouse Road, New Normanton, c.1907. The houses here were inhabited by people like clerks and agents when new in the 1880s. These remain, but the area became very seedy in the post-war years, and only today are signs of revival becoming apparent.

95. St Peter's Church Yard rejoiced in a motley collection of ancient buildings. Shackleton's late medieval shop has already been mentioned (plate 72) and towards the right in this view of 1874 is a very small and ancient cottage. The entire range was destroyed in 1882 except for the *Green Man Inn*, extreme right, with its shaped brick gable. This, however, has been completely gutted by the brewery which owns it.

96. A view down Bold Lane into Jury Street, 25 May 1909. Jury Street was part of the early medieval Jewish quarter of the town. The empty site, left, is where the old *Bird Inn* opposite the end of St Mary's Gate had stood until demolished just before this photograph was taken. Beyond, a shed marks the site of the 1756 Borough Gaol, a very squalid place demolished in 1844. Note the remaining half of a delightful jettied artisan's cottage of late medieval type. This was sacrificed to road widening later in the century.

97. Some houses built for wealthier artisans, like this one opposite St Michael's church in St Michael's Lane, declined into a squalid rookery. Yet slum clearance began late in Derby, not seriously until the 1890s, and many 17th-century brick houses survived into the 1930s in multiple occupation. This view belongs to the 1860s and was taken by Richard Keene. St Alkmund's spire can be seen in the background.

98. Several ranges of late 17th- or early 18th-century cottages survived in the town centre until quite recently and, indeed, one such still stands at the bottom of Green Lane, albeit savaged by conversion into shops. In this view, looking west along the Strand into Cheapside, a particularly charming group survives in the lee of J. S. Story's 1882 Art Gallery. They were demolished after the war to make room for an extension to the Museum, in the event not completed until 1964. Beyond the trees is now a monstrous multi-storey car park; otherwise the scene is little changed.

99. This imposing Regency terrace of four houses behind Friar Gate in Agard Street is in fact eight artisans' cottages built c.1808 for employees at Longdon's mill, opposite, established in 1804. The front doors conceal double entrances *in antis*. This 1960s' photograph shows them in terminal decay; they were demolished in 1975. Agard Street was built by Francis Agard (1760-1820) in 1794, soon after the land was released under the terms of the second Nuns' Green Act. **Agard** was a wealthy mill owner.

100.   Some of the grimmest houses were those built by Alderman Madeley for his workforce at Little City, a small enclave at the south end of Green Lane, in 1806. They were the last of Derby's slums, cleared in the 1950s. This picture was taken for propaganda purposes by the Council in 1946, the mothers and children standing on the corner of Haarlem and Trafalgar Streets.

101. An advance in workers' housing was brought about in 1840-41 by the North Midland Railway, whose architect Francis Thompson built a triangle of remarkably spacious houses, forming a dignified ensemble with his Trijunct station and *Midland Hotel*. They are shown in this 1890s' view, with the then new massive Midland Railway Institute beyond and the hotel in the distance. The cottages were saved from dereliction and imminent destruction in 1980 by the Civic Society and the Derbyshire Historic Buildings Trust, the latter undertaking restoration.

102. It was the impetus of the Midland Railway and the boom in production of narrow tapes, silk and foundry work which followed, that led to the development of New Normanton, consisting of small groups of houses arranged in terraces. Many were designed by W. Willett Popplewell, as here, just beyond *The Cavendish* (*see* plate 74). On the left Walbrook Road creeps towards the site of the future public house, and on the right Cameron Road, also under construction, advances south-westwards. Photograph by Richard Keene, late 1880s.

Inns and Taverns

103.   On a hot day in the late 1930s the *Nottingham Castle Inn*, medieval and later, decays imperceptibly in the sun. It ultimately closed in the late 1950s, lying derelict until demolition in 1964, and the site on the north side of St Michael's Lane became a car park until 1989. The old inn's foundation probably pre-dates the first bridge over the Derwent, *c*.1250, as it takes its name from the traveller's destination as he rode across the Causeway.

104.   Another medieval Derby inn was the *Old White Horse*, Friar Gate, recorded here in one of Richard Keene's most famous images, probably in the 1860s. Here, farmers used to sell produce on the road in front of the inn. Note the sliding York sash above the sign-board, the thatched roofs and the two small cottages beyond. All this was swept away in 1876 when the Great Northern Railway built its line through Derby (Friar Gate). Today the site is occupied by Andrew Handyside's magnificent G.N.R. iron bridge, and the station which closed in the 1960s.

105.   The *Old Dolphin Inn*, Queen Street, claims to have been founded in 1530, and the photograph has been retouched to enhance this impression. The building is plainly of 17th-century date, and the Mercers' Company met there in the 1680s. At some stage it was stuccoed, but the stucco was removed *c*.1902, and the re-exposed timbers decayed swiftly. In this 1930s' photograph the inn has been completely rebuilt. It has subsequently remained unaltered, a pleasant oasis still.

106. The *George* was one of the most famous coaching inns of the 18th century; the façade is visible in plate 78. The rear, shown here in the mid-1850s, was served by George Yard, which plunged through a carriage entrance (left) to emerge into Sadler Gate. The *Chinoiserie* balustraded balcony was thronged in earlier days by guests who could watch entertainments given in the yard below without being jostled by the crowd at ground level. The inn closed in 1850, and the part shown here had become a seedy lodging house offering 'well aired beds' for 3d., 4d. or 6d. The Derby Co-operative Society started in 1850 in an adjacent hay-loft.

107. Very much more in the tavern mould was the *Old Silk Mill* on the north-eastern corner of Full Street, probably contemporary with the building of the Silk Mill itself (*c*.1720). The tavern was pulled down for the building of Sowter Road *c*.1920, and replaced by the present public house of the name. Note the 18th-century cottages, right, sporting two windows paired under one lintel, 'Derby windows'. Silk Mill Lane ran down to the Derwent just off to the right.

108. An early view of Short Street by Richard Keene, taken in the 1860s. This road ran between the north side of Friar Gate and Agard Street, but was later destroyed by the construction of the Great Northern Railway, like the old *White Horse* (no. 104) which stood almost opposite. The tall 18th-century building was the *Lord Hill* tavern, whose landlord was George Jackson. Note the shallow ground-floor windows. It was built in 1793, but must have been named later, after 1814, when Sir Rowland Hill received his peerage.

109. The coming of the *Midland* and *Royal* hotels, and the demise of the stage coaches (the last ran from the *Bell*, Sadler Gate, in 1855), led to a boom in hotel building. The *St James's Hotel* was designed by Giles & Brookhouse and it was built when St James's Lane was widened into St James's Street in 1866. Its façade has since been made into shop fronts, its ballroom is an auction room, and by the 1960s it was merely a town centre inn of dubious reputation. The photograph was taken *c*.1910.

110.   The *Litchurch Inn*, Russell Street, in the heart of the foundry quarter, is shown in this photograph of *c*.1890 with a horse charabanc about to depart for a day out. The inn, built in the 1870s, was named after the medieval township of Litchurch, which became a self-governing settlement in 1860 with its own council and offices, but was re-absorbed by Derby in 1878.

111. A view from the end of Mackworth Road up Cowley Street to distant Kedleston Road, near the junction with Watson Street. The West End streets are alive with people going about their everyday occupations in this turn-of-the-century scene, although the newly-built *Victoria Inn* (grandly called 'Hotel' on the sign) seems deserted: plainly it was not yet opening time.

112. A very grand Edwardian inn for a small suburb: the rebuilt *Coach and Horses* on the corner of **Mansfield Road** and **Old Chester Road**, Little Chester. This attractive edifice – still standing although stripped of some of its ornament by an uncaring brewer – replaced a later 18th-century public house, the predecessor of which, *The Crown*, is marked on Stukeley's map of Little Chester of 1719.

Earning a Living

113.   The Cattle Market and H. I. Stevens' *Corporation Hotel* of 1861 on market day in the years before the First World War. Before 1861 the beast markets had been held at the west end of Friar Gate. In the late 1960s the entire market was re-located at The Meadows, on the opposite side of the river near Nottingham Road, when the new Inner Ring Road was built through its previous site.

114. Derby has been a market town for over a millennium. Here a motley selection of early motor vehicles litter the old wholesale market, built on Meadow Road early in the century to replace previous cramped space adjacent to H. I. Stevens's Cattle Market complex of 1861. This photograph was taken in the mid-1920s.

115. The Morledge Market, c.1926. This ancient thoroughfare represented an overflow from the Market Place, although most stalls were re-located in the new covered market put up on the site of the buildings in the right middle distance in 1933. Some, however, on Cockpit Hill (lower left) survived until the hideous Eagle Centre Market was built in the early 1970s. Note Alexander MacPherson's stylish Edwardian baroque Co-operative building with dome on the left (1914); the Corn Exchange dome, a little to the right; the Guildhall tower, centre background; the Shot Tower; All Saints' tower (the second highest in England); with Cox's lead works and canal basin on the right. The iron *pissoir* – now, regrettably, vanished – is also clearly visible in the foreground.

116.   The mining of alabaster from pits at Chellaston, south of Derby, is an industry which goes back at least to the 15th century. Here the workers at Chellaston's biggest pit pose for an unknown photographer in the 1890s, surrounded by blocks of the attractive soft stone with its locally characteristic rusty veining. The last pit was filled with waste from the 1960s.

117.   Brickmaking was another local industry, practised as centrally as Nuns' Green in the 17th century. One of the most productive brickworks was at Rowditch, on the Uttoxeter Road, owned in the 18th century by Abraham Denstone. On his death it passed to a remote cadet line of the Harpurs of Calke, becoming part of a larger local combine by the 20th century. This view looking east shows the area in 1931. Today a Sainsbury's superstore occupies the site, successor to an industrial rubbish tip.

118. The Derby Silk Mill from Silk Mill Lane, which ran east from Full Street, photographed by Richard Keene in the 1860s. The mill was built by George Sorocold for John Lombe in 1717-18, and claims to have been the first factory in England. The wrought-iron gate was by Robert Bakewell (*c*.1724), and has survived almost on the same spot, as has the tower. The cottages were demolished to make way for an electricity power station in the 1920s, the site of which now houses a modern transformer compound surrounded by a high brick wall.

119. In 1910 the silk mill burned down – this photograph was taken on the morning after the fire. It was rebuilt three storeys high instead of five, and survives as the Derby Industrial Museum. The hipped roof visible in this view and the previous one was put on in the early 19th century; originally the roof had been flat with a parapet. The other original part of Lombe's mill, the doubling shop, lay to the left, out of view, but collapsed in 1893. The island was bigger two centuries earlier, and supported a large tower-like monument and a forest of obelisks; these have never been satisfactorily explained.

120. Pot Works House, built for William Butts, the Cockpit Hill Pottery master potter in 1750. It is pictured here in 1921, in decay. Siddal's Road runs to the left *en route* for the station; Cockpit Hill itself lies to the right. The pot works, which mainly made earthenware, closed when the banker John Heath went bankrupt in March 1779. The house was then divided as tenements. The site of the pot works itself was swiftly built over. This was probably also the site of Derby's Castle, thought to have been an adulterine one built by the Earls of Chester in the 1130s.

121. Cox's lead works in 1932, the year the complex was demolished to make way for the present Corporation Street and the Council House. The Shot Tower was added in 1809 (built by Joseph Gascoyne) and was a famous landmark for five generations of Derby people. The opulent Cox family, originally from Brailsford, were not only lead merchants and smelters but also successful vintners: a strange combination upon which to make a fortune!

122. Midland Place in 1874. Bemrose's new printing works had just been completed in this Richard Keene photograph. Note the second-grade terrace of North Midland Railway cottages on the right. Bemrose's had been established in 1822 on Irongate and this was their first large-scale expansion; more of the building lies, out of view, in Wellington Street. In the distance is Calvert Street and, beyond the wall, the Derby Canal.

123. A newspaper stall in the Market Hall, with staff and customers posing for the camera, in the 1920s. The stalls were all replaced by more up-to-date structures in the late 1930s, and again in the current refurbishment, 1989.

124. The Star Tea Co. was a large firm in its day, having three depôts, as well as an outlet at 13, St Peter's Street. This was rebuilt in heroic style by Edwin Thompson in 1874, due to street widening. This photograph of the St Peter's Street staff predates that event, however. Note the delightful cast-iron window, left, with gothic glazing bars.

THE GREAT ATTRACTION IN DERBY IS THE

MIDLAND · DRAPERY · COMPANY

☞ VISITORS TO DERBY SHOULD
SEE THE GREAT ATTRACTION

Smartest and most up-to-date Shops
and Showrooms in the Midlands ::

37, 39, 41, 43, ST. PETER'S STREET, &
1, 2, 3, 4, 5, 6, 7, 8, 9, EAST STREET,
DERBY

FRONTAGE OF THREE HUNDRED AND FORTY-FIVE FEET

THE · MIDLAND · DRAPERY · COMPANY

37, 39, 41, 43, ST. PETER'S STREET, and 1, 2, 3, 4, 5, 6, 7, 8, 9, EAST STREET, DERBY

Telegrams : "ANN, DERBY"   THE FAVOURITE CASH DRAPERS   Telephone : 288 DERBY

☞ VISITORS TO DERBY SHOULD SEE THE GREAT ATTRACTION ☜

125. An exceedingly imaginative perspective of the newly-built Midland Drapery store, from a woodcut of 1891. Started by Alderman Sir Edwin Ann (d.1913) in 1882, this grandiose complex was built 1887-92, probably to the designs of Arthur Coke-Hill. To the left is the St Peter's Street frontage, with its well-remembered inverted horseshoe magnet on the top at the corner. The East Street frontage was normally only visible at an oblique angle, as the street was barely 20 feet wide. Nor was the shop completed as shown. It was demolished c.1970.

126.   Cockpit Hill showing The Hay and Corn Stores, photographed in 1921. This range of buildings survived until 1971, but it would be difficult to purchase a hay bale in Derby today.

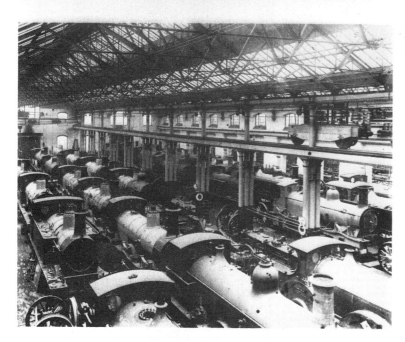

127. The erecting shop at Midland Railway locomotive works in the 1880s; photograph by Keene or Thomas Scotton, his successor.

128. The interior of one of the smaller Derby foundries, probably Smith Bros. of Abbey Street or Abell's in 1907. The coming of the railways led to the establishment of heavy industry in Derby, especially ironfounding. Products were mainly railway components or domestic grates and ranges, although there were some specialist firms, like John and James Fox (lathes and machine tools), Haslam's (refrigeration machinery) and Fletcher's (sugar refining equipment).

129.   Outside the Rolls-Royce works in Nightingale Road (built 1907). This photograph shows Rolls-Royce families' day in July 1919. The Hon C. S. Rolls was a great pioneer of aviation but after he was killed flying in 1910 Sir Henry Royce turned his back on aviation until the Great War led to Rolls-Royce building aero-engines. Car production was shifted to Crewe in 1945, leaving Derby to concentrate solely on aero-engine production.

130.   Two great industries came to Derby in the early 20th century – Rolls-Royce in 1907 and, shortly afterwards, Courtauld's, later British Celanese. This 1920s' scene shows part of the workforce heading home across the railway line at Spondon station on a winter evening. The then newly-built *Station Inn* can be seen in the background. Undoubtedly, a good number of the people in the picture would be turning right to catch a train into Derby; few would have lived in the then small village of Spondon in those days. Spondon was absorbed into the Borough of Derby in 1968.

131. The agent posing with eight members of the outdoor staff of Darley Hall, then the seat of the mill-owning Evans family, in the 1890s.

132. From 1860 until 1877, when it was incorporated into Derby, the former hamlet of Litchurch was, in effect, a self-governing town, the population swollen by ironfounding from a few hundred in 1810 to something like 50,000. It had its own council, officers and services, and enjoyed lower rates than Derby. Here, in a famous photograph of 1873, is its fire brigade, outside Sir Gilbert Scott's church, vicarage and school of St Andrew, London Road, then but a decade old.

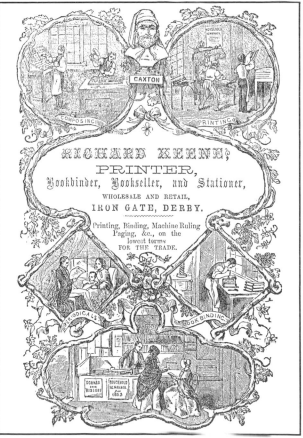

133. Richard Keene and John Alfred Warwick taking photographs with friends in Dovedale in the 1870s. Keene (1825-94) was apprenticed as a bookseller, printer and stationer. In 1848 he set up on his own (see his advertisement plate for 1853, right), moving to a house in Irongate a few years later. Keene's interest in photography was roused by Rev. Edward Abney of The Firs, a friend of Fox-Talbot. Keene took up photography with his friend Warwick (a telegraph engineer on the Midland Railway), at first as a hobby, but from the mid-1950s professionally. In 1855 and again in 1858 he and Warwick toured the Peak District, taking views which, with those they took of Derby, formed the backbone of Keene's subsequent catalogue. At the same time, he undertook to photograph the seats of the Derbyshire gentry, a valuable record.

Transport

134.   The first turnpike roads through Derby opened in 1756 (to Chesterfield) and 1758 (to London via Shardlow). Nearly all of Derby's surviving toll houses have now been restored. This one, demolished about the turn of the century, stood on the Ashbourne Road (part of an early turnpike to Manchester via Ashbourne) near Markeaton Lane. It would appear from its design to date to *c*.1800, and perhaps replaced an earlier wooden house. Note the locally-made cast-iron gothick windows in this 1870s' view.

135.   An Edwardian mail van in the yard of the G.P.O., St James's Street, *c*.1905.

136. The Derby Canal, which ran from the Trent and Mersey to Little Eaton and east to the Erewash canal, opened in 1796. The Cockpit Hill canal basin in Derby was graced from 1820 by the elegant Bridgewater warehouse, operated by Pickfords. It is shown here in decay in the late 1930s, with rusted derrick, sunken butty and contented swan. It survived until 1977, long after the canal itself had been filled in.

137. The canal crossed the Derwent on the flat, the river being maintained at the correct height between two weirs, and the towpath crossed on a narrow wooden bridge called the Long Bridge. In this 1950s' view, it had been closed as unsafe, and was demolished in 1959. The view is from the east bank (called Canary Island) looking towards Cockpit Hill. To the left is the south weir, the gables of the 1861 wholesale market (by H. I. Stevens and George Thompson) and the ice factory. To the right can be seen part of the bus station and the commencement of the Riverside Gardens, on the site of the lead works.

138.   Three railway companies – North Midland, Midland Counties and Birmingham and Derby Junction – opened in 1839-40, building a joint station south of the town to the designs of Francis Thompson, with a single platform over 1,000 ft. in length. This lithograph was produced at the time for the *British Gazetteer*. It was an extremely dignified and competent piece of late classical architecture.

139.   In 1844 the original three railway companies amalgamated to form the Midland Railway, which survived until 1 January 1923. The station was extended, the façade twice – in 1869, by J.H. Sanders, who added this *porte cochère* to Thompson's façade, and in 1892, when Charles Trubshaw extended the frontage forward, moving the *porte cochère* to match, as shown here *c.*1908. All was demolished, with the connivance of the City and County Councils, in 1984, although Thompson's original façade was briefly revealed in the process. The pediment and clock survive, built incongruously into a car park wall.

140.   The first locomotive engineer of the Midland Railway was Matthew Kirtley (1813-73). He is depicted here in the late 1860s, at his residence, Litchurch Grange, with his wife Ann in the window, and daughters Elizabeth Ann (born 1842) and Emily, later Lady Roe (born 1845), standing. The house was an ancient one, rebuilt *c*.1840, and bought from the Morris family by Kirtley in the later 1860s; previously they had lived on Burton Road.

141.   The locomotives built for the Midland Railway had remarkably long lives. In this photograph an ex-Midland Railway 2P 4-4-0 in British Railways livery pauses near Francis Thompson's North Midland Railway Roundhouse in the early 1950s.

142. The horse omnibus came to Derby about the same time as the railway, thanks to William Wallace Wallis, whose father George had kept the *New Inn*. By 1899, services were in the hands of the new County Borough undertaking. Here one of their horse buses prepares to leave from John Ward's newly-erected Tramways Offices in Victoria Street, *c*.1905. Note the rudimentary seats on the open and flimsily protected upper deck and the beautifully made coachwork, decorated at the corners with stylised lotus petals. Three horses draw the bus, and the Athenaeum Club and *Royal Hotel* form an impressive backdrop.

143. An early horse omnibus belonging to the Derby Tramways Company at the Deadman's Lane depot, before setting off for Alvaston. Note that there was a flat rate fare of 2d. The picture was taken in the 1880s. Edgar Horne, the music shop proprietor whose advertisement can be seen on the vehicle, later became Mayor of Derby. Deadman's Lane, once the site of a plague pit, was the stop for those who worked at the Midland Railway's carriage and wagon works.

144. A view up Cornmarket, *c.*1889, looking north from St Peter's Bridge. Cabs wait, then as now, in the left foreground. The horse trams were introduced in 1880, taken over by the Corporation in 1899, and electrified from 1904. Albert House, extreme right, was built in 1848 when Albert Street was constructed from Victoria Street to Tenant Street Bridge.

145. The inauguration of the electric tramways, 26 July 1904. An eager throng gathers around two cars at the then southernmost point of the network, Upper Dale Road. The trams and the road had not yet reached *The Cavendish*. Old Normanton village and the spire of St Giles's church, rebuilt nearly 40 years before by Giles & Brookhouse, are faintly visible on the distant ridge. The man in the light fedora is the Mayor, Alderman Cornelius Boam; behind him is the chairman of the tramways committee, the Hon. Frederick Strutt (Mayor in 1902), Lord Belper's youngest son.

146.   After the electrification of the tramways from 1904, a new depôt was opened on the other side of the Carriage and Wagon Works, on Osmaston Road, near the Hall. In this First World War view of the interior, the maintenance workers pose with one of their charges.

147.   Soon the electric trams were operating on the majority of main roads. Here, at Five Lamps – so named from the impressive standard brought here from the Cornmarket shortly before – a tram emerges past the 18th-century Elms from Kedleston Road. Straight ahead is the Duffield Road (*see* plate 26), the old road north as re-aligned by turnpiking in the 18th century. The Five Lamps have long since gone, but the name has been retained.

148. Horse charabancs had given way to motor ones by the 1920s. Here a solid-tyred example is about to depart from Longdon's mill in Agard Street in 1923 with a party of employees bound for North Wales. Longdon's has now closed, but the mill survives.

149. Osmaston Road at the junction with Douglas Street early in the afternoon of 21 February 1928, looking north. Edward, Prince of Wales, is about to pass, *en route* for Rolls-Royce; the street is full of people and the police are keeping a high profile. By the end of the Great War the Derby tramcars had all acquired roofs to their upper decks.

150. In 1932 the first trolleybus appeared, displacing the trams within two years. Here, an early trolleybus pauses on the north side of the Market Place in 1949. In the background on the right is Tenant Street; the large building was by G. H. Sheffield but was demolished in 1987 to make way for a hotel. Cars were parked in the centre of the Market Place from 1932 until 1973.

151. Trolleybuses, which continued in use until 1967, were renowned for their speed, quietness, and non-polluting nature. Their disadvantage was that they were not flexible – a change in route demanded major engineering works. They also broke down from time to time, as this 1950s' photograph reveals! Six employees were needed to get this 'dead' trolleybus moving, even downhill, in the Osmaston Road area.

152.   From 1932, the old lead works site on The Morledge was cleared to make way for the Town Centre Development Scheme. One of the first fruits of this was the very modern bus station, cleverly shoehorned into a limited, curving site. To its left is the new open market, replacing the Market Place; both were designed by C. H. Aslin, the Borough Architect. Beyond is the cattle market and *Corporation Hotel* (centre right). This photograph was taken in 1933. The site in the foreground, now Wakefield's Army Stores, then housed a circus.

153.   In 1938 Derby Corporation opened an airfield on a former Mosley family estate at Burnaston, the elegant post-Soanian villa serving as terminal building and clubhouse. This picture shows police and fire officers who have just been up in a DH89 Dragon Rapide, evaluating the potential of aviation in their work. The airport was replaced by the East Midlands Airport, Castle Donnington, and closed to all but club flying in 1972. The house was sold and nearly fell down, but by 1988 a restoring owner had been found. In April 1989 it was decided that the airfield should be the site for a new Toyota car factory, and the County Council supported a successful application to demolish all buildings on the site.

Special Events

154.   The Royal Agricultural Show was sometimes held on Osmaston Park, so Derby was frequently host to royal visitors. This view of the mysteriously-named 'Spot' (where the Osmaston Road and London Road turnpikes of 1758 diverged) shows the triumphal arch erected for the Prince and Princess of Wales to pass through on their way to open the show, 15 July 1881. T. H. Bennett's shop on the left, with the large Union Flag, was renowned for dealing in tea and issued small bronze trade tokens in the 1850s. The scene is much changed today.

155.   For the Royal Show, a portable prefabricated pavilion was designed and used from the 1870s until the Second World War when it vanished for good. It is shown here in June 1906. The frontage faced London Road. The show, held on Osmaston Park, was opened by King Edward VII who unveiled a statue to his mother at The Spot on the same occasion.

156.   Laying the foundation stone of the rebuilt St Peter's church, 1898, by the Bishop of Southwell. Derby was in the diocese of Southwell until 1927. The tower was rebuilt from the ground up, as was the west part of the nave and the chancel. The nave was extended to the west by one bay; the architect was W. Hawley Lloyd.

157.   The junction of London Road and Midland Road, 1899. A unit of the Sherwood Foresters marches towards the station to entrain for the coast and the South African War, surrounded by an enthusiastic mob. The new building in the background is the Salvation Army hostel. To the right are two public houses, the *Nottingham Arms* (presently shut and boarded up) and the *Leviathan* (long since vanished).

158. In 1989 Derby appointed a town crier, the first for 120 years. The last one prior to that had been Joseph Parr (1790-1868), 'Pindar and common crier of Derby', depicted here in a daguerrotype of *c.*1859. He lived in St Alkmund's Church Yard, and was a descendant of a decayed branch of a family which had rented space in the Shambles since 1540, and had produced a mayor in 1723.

159. A scene near the railway station on 22 April 1865, when Miss Wilmot of Chaddesden Hall launched the new *Florence Nightingale* lifeboat, paid for by subscription raised in the town and presented to the R.N.L.I. for use at Sunderland. The photograph is by W. W. Winter.

160.   The Alexandra Ice Rink was founded in 1863 and built on the corner of Normanton Road and Hartington Street. This photograph shows it after conversion to roller skating about the turn of the century, with some members of a band present. It was converted by Thomas Harrison Thorpe into a cinema in 1913 and was destroyed by fire after reconversion from a Bingo Hall to retail use in 1982. It reverted briefly to being a roller skating emporium in the 1950s.

161.   Regattas started on the Derwent in the early 19th century, ceased for 40 years or so and were revived 1857-78. The Derby Rowing Club revived the regattas permanently in 1880. This view shows the 1907 event under way, looking north from Handyside's G.N.R. bridge, with part of Darley Park visible on the left. The trees on the right hide Derwent Farm, one of Little Chester's two surviving prebendal farms.

162. Fun fair on the Morledge, Easter 1913. The fairs were banished to the south of the town in the 1920s, but since the Second World War have taken place on Bass's Recreation Ground, not far from their original site.

163. The Derby Art Gallery was designed by John Soames Story and opened in 1882. It is shown here in 1912 with an exhibition of Italian old masters, on loan from the Drury-Lowe family of nearby Locko Park. The room is now the Joseph Wright gallery. Today there is a doorway on the left into the natural history gallery and, at the point where the rope starts, a stair rises to the temporary exhibition galleries, both put in when a new extension to the museum was opened in 1964. The lighting and plush bench seating have vanished.

164. Alderman William Blews Robotham was Mayor of Derby at the time of the signing of the Versailles Treaty in 1919 and issued a medallion to celebrate the final end of hostilities. When he laid down office in November that year (modern mayors retire in May), a formal dinner was held in his honour at the *Royal Hotel*, in the Athenaeum suite, shown here at the speech stage. The good Alderman is in the background to the right of his successor, Alderman Eggleston (with walrus moustache and chain) who presided.

165. A full, formal, Mayoral visit to the Baptist church, St Mary's Gate, for the Royal Infirmary Free Churches Annual Service, 27 April 1921. Note the halberdiers, C. J. Shackleton (Serjeant at Mace) sword bearer and Town Clerk, with dignitaries and aldermen grouped on the perron behind, almost obscuring Bakewell's ironwork. The Mayor is Alderman Dr. Robert Laurie (d.1929).

166. St Alkmund's parish dressed St Alkmund's Well in Well Street (off North Parade) from 1870 until war curtailed the ceremony in 1939. It was never revived after the war, and the church closed in 1966, although the citizens of Little Chester revived well-dressing at their two Roman wells in 1980. This photograph was taken on Whit Sunday 1926, and shows the St Alkmund's Well dressed in traditional fashion, those who created it standing proudly before their handiwork.

167. On the night of 21-22 May 1932, the Markeaton Brook flooded violently, the worst since 1 April 1842. Much damage was done to shop stock, largely stored in basements. Here a group of young people, photographed by Hurst and Wallace, seem to be enjoying themselves in Victoria Street, outside Woolworths which was then opposite the *Royal Hotel*. The Brook was subsequently rebuilt to prevent further floods, along lines suggested by Herbert Spencer after the 1842 flood! So far, the arrangements have been effective.

Sport and Recreation

168. Allenton Boys' football team, season 1926-27.

169. The first XI cricket team of Derby School posed outside Percy Currey's chapel at St Helen's, 1939.

170.   Temple House was one of an important group of Regency villas designed by Alderman Richard Leaper (1759-1838), a gifted amateur, for his friends. It was adapted for a special school in the 1930s by Derby Borough Council, and some of the children are shown here enjoying outdoor classes in June 1936. The school closed and the house was destroyed in the 1960s.

171.   Rev. Edward Abney's estate nearby at The Firs was sold off and developed for housing in the later 19th century. The Board school on Leman Street, later called Firs Estate, was opened about 1890. A physical training class is seen in progress in this 1920s view.

172.   There have been many private academies in Derby, from that founded by Herbert Spencer's grandfather right through to the present. This view of *c.*1912 shows some of the girls of Belmont School playing tennis in the garden. The school occupied No. 99 Friar Gate, a very fine house built for the Hurt family around 1750, and still extant. Shortly after this photograph was taken the school moved to more spacious premises and the house became the home of Dr. T. H. Bennett, organist of All Saints'. He installed an organ in the sitting room and also ran a musical academy.

173.   Alvaston Park Lake, on a summer's day around 1931. This 30-acre park was created for the Corporation by Barrons in 1913, although the lake was not added until a decade later. A branch Carnegie Library was also built at the edge of the park in 1916, but this was demolished in 1980.

174. The 100-acre park at Markeaton, having been taken over by the Corporation in 1929, was modified in various ways to enhance its appeal to the public. The lake, part of William Emes's landscaping, was enlarged to facilitate boating, and the Mundy play area and paddling pool were created in the early 1930s. This view shows the pool in use shortly after it opened. The hill behind is now covered with housing, marking the westwards expansion of the suburb of Allestree after the war.

Suburbs

175.   Allestree is a pleasant village on the A6, the road north from Derby. The village expanded crazily in the 1950s and 1960s, at a cost to some traditional buildings. This is James Wyatt's Home Farm, which fell to the developer in 1972. Mercifully, his Allestree Hall has survived and, despite threats in the 1970s, is only one of two larger seats to have been spared from demolition by the City Council.

176.   As Derby became more sulphurous in the early 19th century, so its leading citizens moved out to the suburbs, building pleasing Regency villas to live in. This is Nunsfield House, a beautifully proportioned example in the former village of Boulton, south of Derby. It was built c.1830 for Charles Holbrooke, a lead merchant. Today it is very dilapidated, and is owned by the County Council.

177. Chaddesden lies over the Derwent, on a low ridge to the east of the City, becoming built up from the 1920s. The sale of the Wilmot family's house and estate there greatly facilitated the process; the hall, built in the manner of Francis Smith of Warwick and given a new central bay *c.*1800, was demolished in 1926. It is shown here in the time of Sir Henry Wilmot, 5th Bt., V.C., K.C.B. (1831-1901) in a Keene photograph taken about 1860. Part of the park survives for public recreation.

178. To the north of Derby, between Allestree and the Derwent, lies Darley, from the 1150s to 1538 Derbyshire's largest monastic site. From its ruins, Robert Sacheverell built Darley Hall, replaced in 1727 for William Woolley the younger by Francis Smith of Warwick. Joseph Pickford added wings north and south for the Holdens. The Evanses, the cotton spinners who practically built the village from 1782, left Darley Hall to the Borough in 1925 along with its dramatic park by William Emes. The house was demolished in 1962 for no good reason. This photograph shows Smith's east front in the 1920s.

179.   Abutting the Darley Hall estate was the smaller park of Derwent Bank, a large house of 1811 designed by amateur architect and four times Mayor of Derby, Alderman Richard Leaper (1759-1838) for Thomas Bridgett, a rich silk throwster. This painting, by one of the Misses Strutt who lived there from the 1830s, shows the interior of the artist's sitting room. In the late 19th century much of the park was built over, and the house was demolished in 1924.

180.   Littleover, west of the town, was part of the manor of Mickleover, historically a holding of Burton Abbey. Littleover Hollow, with its picturesque timber-framed 16th-century cottage, was a favourite location for photographers and painters alike. The cottage survives today although the encroachment of modern housing has all but ruined the scene. This photograph was taken around 1900.

181.   Littleover also boasted a house by Alderman Leaper, constructed for Josias Cockshutt in 1808 and altered in 1827. It incorporated a vast stone Jacobean overmantel from Littleover Hall, installed when the Heathcotes, previously of the Hall, inherited this house from Cockshutt's heiress. Sir Abraham Woodiwiss greatly enlarged the house in matching style without, but in ornate Jacobethan style within in 1881, the whole being set in a small but very beautiful park. Mercifully, The Pastures survives, albeit somewhat mauled by the Health Authority.

182. Francis Noel Clarke Mundy (1739-1815) was the social mainspring behind Derby's vigorous intellectual and cultural life in the later 18th century. He inherited a new house built in 1755 by James Denstone for his father. Denstone was brother of Pickford's *stuccadore*. Mundy had Emes landscape the 100-acre park and Pickford designed the pretty orangery, seen on the left in this 1930s' photograph of the west front. The house, Markeaton Hall, and much of the park was given to the Borough by the last Mrs. Mundy in 1929, but the house was demolished in 1964 after years of neglect, the park brutalised and the surviving orangery and stabling mutilated.

183. Mickleover bestrides the Uttoxeter Road, three miles from Derby. It began to be 'suburbanised' after 1876, when the Great Northern Railway's extension was built from Derby via Mickleover to Eggington Junction. This photograph, taken about 1900, shows pupils standing in front of the village school. The school closed about a decade ago but fortunately the pretty building of 1897 or so survives.

184. The centre of Mickleover village is called The Square, and is shown here on 14 October 1930, looking westwards along the Uttoxeter Road. Most of the buildings, including the *Masons' Arms* in the distance, survive, although there are currently plans afoot to build houses in the small park of Mickleover Manor (designed by Thomas Barron) over the wall in the far distance. Note the unusual iron drinking fountain in the centre of the square, now vanished.

185. The charming medieval church of Normanton-by-Derby photographed by Richard Keene about 1858. It is likely that the delightful weathercock was a fabrication of Robert Bakewell's, but it was lost along with almost all the old church when Giles & Brookhouse got to work to build a new St Giles' church here within the decade, as a response to the increase in numbers of local residents. This was caused by the expansion of New Normanton, between this village and the southern edge of the Borough.

186. The expansion of New Normanton soon swept away most of the older farmsteads lying in its way. This one, Peartree Farm, was run by John and Ann Peach until the former's death in 1861 (about the date of the photograph) when it was sold, and gave its name to a street and a whole area of New Normanton. Harrington Street now runs across the front of the picture. The early 18th-century farmhouse is unusual, being built of keuper sandstone as well as brick, and the uneven fenestration suggests an earlier core.

187. Another church which has now vanished was that of St James, Osmaston-by-Derby, again originally medieval, although largely rebuilt in the 1870s. This unique picture shows it before that time, however. The village at Osmaston virtually disappeared after William Emes landscaped the Hall parkland in 1789. The Midland Railway bought the estate in 1888, and began expanding the works over it.

188. In 1938 Osmaston Hall (*above*) passed into Council ownership and was sacrificed to housing and, after the war, an industrial estate. The house had originally been built in 1696 for a branch of the Wilmots of Chaddesden to the designs of Sir William Wilson (1641-1710). By 1860, when this photograph was taken by Richard Keene, it had been let to the wealthy Fox family of Derby. The photograph (*right*) shows Corporation workmen beginning demolition in 1938.

Some Derby People

189. Mr. and Mrs. Tattershaw with their young son, pot boy and two engaging pets posing outside the *Globe Tavern*, *c*.1900. The *Globe* in Sacheverell Street (which runs between Osmaston Road and Normanton Road) was merely a beer house until an Act of 1906 enabled it to broaden its appeal. It closed about 1975 and the site was cleared.

190. Sir Alfred Seale Haslam, the Mayor, examines preparations for the royal visit of 1891, when Queen Victoria laid the foundation stone of the Royal Infirmary. He is depicted next to one of the unfinished triumphal arches (which he had paid for himself) decorating the royal route. This one was outside the Midland Railway Station and gives an interesting insight into the construction of these extravagant masterpieces.

191. A postcard published by the Associated Society of Railway Servants in the Edwardian period showing a group of Midland Railway guards sacked as a result of the 1911 strike (led by A. E. Waterson, A.S.R.S. General Secretary and later a Labour M.P.). The profits of the cards (1d. each) were to go to help Messrs. W. Jenkinson, D. Cadman, J. Ewins (back row, left to right) and J. Cutts, W. J. Short, G. H. Dalley (front row, left to right) whilst unemployed.

192.   Mrs. Adolphus Grimwood-Taylor, wife of the County under-sheriff, in her sitting room at No. 36, St Mary's Gate, still one of Derby's finest early 18th-century town houses. It was built for the Bateman family of Hertington Hall in 1729-31, and by the 1770s had passed to the Simpsons, solicitors. The partnership they founded still occupies the building, although the senior partner's family has moved since this photograph was taken in the early years of the century.

MAP
OF
THE BOROUGH OF
DERBY,
LITCHURCH, AND
NEW NORMANTON
BY
BEMROSE & SONS.

1876

Reference.

Ward and Township Boundaries ....
Municipal Boundary _____
Parliamentary do 1868 _ _ _ _ _ _ _
The figures thus 214·8 denote in feet and decimals the mean level of the Sea at Liverpool

SCALES.

LITTLEOVER

NORMANTON

☩ Normanton Church

☩ Osmaston Church